Dear Parent:
Your child's love of reading starts here!

Every child learns to read in a different way and at his or her own speed. Some go back and forth between reading levels and read favorite books again and again. Others read through each level in order. You can help your young reader improve and become more confident by encouraging his or her own interests and abilities. From books your child reads with you to the first books he or she reads alone, there are I Can Read Books for every stage of reading:

SHARED READING
Basic language, word repetition, and whimsical illustrations, ideal for sharing with your emergent reader

BEGINNING READING
Short sentences, familiar words, and simple concepts for children eager to read on their own

READING WITH HELP
Engaging stories, longer sentences, and language play for developing readers

READING ALONE
Complex plots, challenging vocabulary, and high-interest topics for the independent reader

ADVANCED READING
Short paragraphs, chapters, and exciting themes for the perfect bridge to chapter books

I Can Read Books have introduced children to the joy of reading since 1957. Featuring award-winning authors and illustrators and a fabulous cast of beloved characters, I Can Read Books set the standard for beginning readers.

A lifetime of discovery begins with the magical words **"I Can Read!"**

Visit www.icanread.com for information
on enriching your child's reading experience.

I Can Read Book® is a trademark of HarperCollins Publishers.

Danny and the Dinosaur and the Sand Castle Contest
Copyright © 2018 by Anti-Defamation League Foundation, The Authors Guild Foundation, ORT America, Inc., United Negro College Fund, Inc.

Library of Congress Control Number: 2017956222
ISBN 978-0-06-241049-8 (trade bdg.) — ISBN 978-0-06-241048-1 (pbk.)

Typography by Jeff Shake
18 19 20 21 22   SCP   10 9 8 7 6 5 4 3 2 1   ❖   First Edition

I Can Read!

BEGINNING 1 READING

Syd Hoff's

DANNY AND THE DINOSAUR

and the Sand Castle Contest

Written by Bruce Hale

Illustrated in the style of Syd Hoff by Charles Grosvenor

HARPER

An Imprint of HarperCollins Publishers

"We're going to the beach tomorrow,"
Danny told his friend the dinosaur.
"Would you like to come along?"

"I'd love to," said the dinosaur.

"What's a beach?"

Danny smiled.

"It's lots of fun!"

5

The next day, Danny's parents
packed the car with towels
and treats.
Danny and his friend Betty
climbed in.

They all drove to the beach
while the dinosaur followed behind.

It was a beautiful day at the beach.

Everyone was playing,

swimming, and sunbathing.

8

The dinosaur loved it.

He splashed in the waves
and rolled on the sand.

"The beach is the best!" he said.

"Hey, look," said Betty.

"It's the sand castle contest."

"I know," said Danny.

"I've entered, but I've never won.

I've been thinking

about this since last summer!"

"Maybe this is your lucky year,"

said the dinosaur.

"I'll help you."

"How can we lose?" said Danny.

10

Danny and Betty started to dig.

The dinosaur dug too,

but he was a little too helpful.

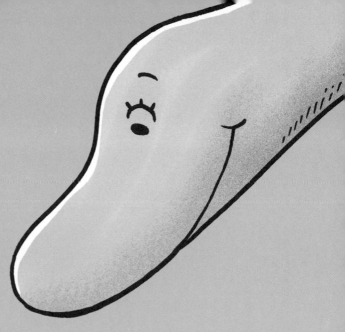

"We need water to wet the sand,"
said Danny.

"No problem," said the dinosaur.

At last, the castle was almost done.

"This is my best ever!" said Danny.

"Let's pack down the sand."

"Let me do it," said the dinosaur.

The dinosaur packed a bit too hard.

"Oops," he said. "I'm so sorry!"

"My castle!" cried Danny.

16

"The judging starts in ten minutes," said the announcer.

"OH, NO!" cried Danny and Betty.

"What do we do now?"

Danny looked at the dinosaur.

He looked at the ocean.

"I've got it," he said.

"But we'll need some help."

"What can I do?" the dinosaur asked.

"Just lie down," said Danny.

19

With the help of some new friends,

Danny and Betty piled sand

all over the dinosaur.

They added waves and fins.

They made a sand sea monster!

"We will win for sure!" said Betty.

Everyone agreed it was the best.

"Thanks, guys!" said Danny.

But then, Danny noticed something.

The tide was coming in.

Everyone's castles were in danger!

"Can you hold back the tide?"

Danny asked the dinosaur.

"I can," said his friend.

"But what about your sea monster?"
said Betty.

"Saving our friends' sand castles
is more important," said Danny.

The dinosaur shook off the sand.

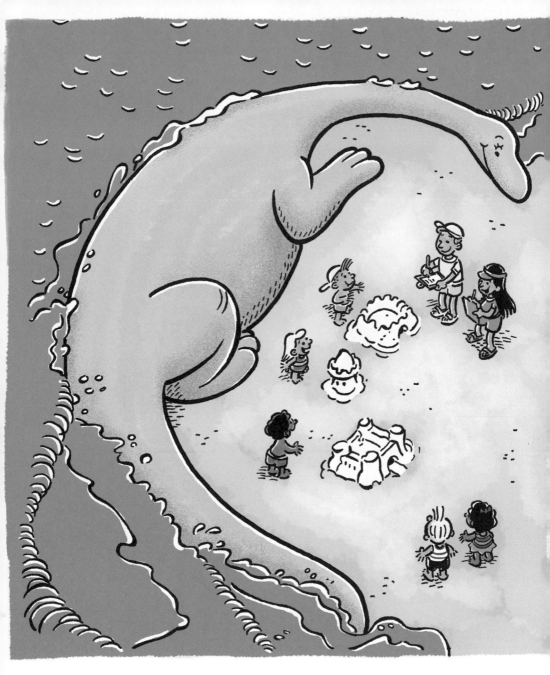

He blocked the waves

while the judges finished judging.

"Hooray for Danny and the dinosaur!"
everyone cheered.

"You didn't win," said Betty.

"But I made new friends," said Danny.

"And I'll try again next year."

The dinosaur took all
the new friends swimming.
Everyone played in the waves.

At the end of the day
everyone celebrated with Popsicles.
And the dinosaur had
the biggest one of all!